Katrina and Winter: Partners in Courage

by
Nancy Stewart

This book is dedicated to Katrina Simpkins, my hero,
who at her tender age has taught me much about a life well lived.

Katrina and Winter: Partners in Courage
Copyright © 2012 Nancy Stewart
Photos Copyright © 2012 Maria Simpkins
Hardcover ISBN: 9781616332426; 1616332425
Paperback ISBN: 9781616332433; 1616332433
eBook ISBN: 9781616332440; 1616332441
April 2012
Published in the United States of America

Library of Congress Control Number: 2012937189

GUARDIAN ANGEL PUBLISHING, INC.
12430 Tesson Ferry Road #186
Saint Louis, Missouri 63128 USA
http://www.GuardianAngelPublishing.com

Chapter 1
A DOLPHIN SURPRISE

"I can't wait to see everything!" eight year old Katrina shouted. Palm trees seemed to speed by the car window. She gathered her hair into a ponytail. "Know what?" she asked her parents in the front seat. "I won't mind using my helper leg. It'll be crowded at Disney World, and no one's gonna notice." *I hope,* she thought.

"That's the spirit, sweetheart," her mom answered, pushing up her glasses. "Remember the aquarium I read about in Clearwater? Maybe we should go. You  kids haven't been to one, and it's not very far out of the way."

Katrina frowned. "Aw no, Mom. I want to get to Disney and not stop at a dumb aquarium."

"Let's do it!" her older sister, Sara, urged. "Come on, K. It'll be fun. Something different."

Katrina scowled at her sister and let out a long breath. "This'll be so uncool. A bunch of fish."

As they drove toward the aquarium, Katrina began to get nervous, the way she always did in new surroundings. She felt a thin sheen of sweat above her lip in spite of the car's chilled air.

That place won't be crowded, I bet, and people are gonna notice me. I hate wearing this helper leg. She felt tears pinprick behind her eyes. She knew they were going to spill over, so she turned away from Sara. *When people stare or point, I want to cry.* Katrina wiped sweaty palms on her pink capris. *Not being normal's the worst.*

"Here it is, guys," her dad said, breaking into Katrina's troubled thoughts. He turned into the Clearwater Marine Aquarium parking lot and found a space.

She stepped out into brilliant sunlight and looked around. *Parking lot's not very crowded, but maybe more people will come soon.* Entering the building, Katrina said, "What's with this place? It's tiny. I don't see any fish, either."

A man walked up to Katrina and her family. He had a friendly smile and thin grey hair. "You're right, young lady. This is a marine animal rescue aquarium." He pointed to his badge. "We treat sick or wounded sea animals. If possible, they're released back to their homes."

Katrina raised her eyebrows. "Oh, I didn't know that."

"Yeah," he answered. "There's lots to see here, but no fish!"

Around a corner of the lobby, she noticed a large aquarium window. Through it she saw an animal that looked unusual.

"Is that a dolphin with a stump instead of a tail?" she asked the volunteer.

He nodded. "Yes, that's Winter. She's a very special dolphin. Everybody's favorite."

"Can I see her?" she asked.

Pointing to the stairs, he said, "Sure. Let's go."

Katrina let the volunteer take the lead, not wanting him to see her walk up steps. She slowly climbed the stairs. *How can Winter swim without a tail? Maybe the way I walk without a leg?*

At the top of the stairs a huge deck wrapped around the tanks, partly shaded by tent material.

"Lots of tanks up here," Sara said.

The man nodded. "Yes, we have sea turtles and dolphins that can't be returned to the wild in these tanks. Unfortunately, some sea turtles are hit by boat propellers or get tangled in fishing nets."

"I didn't know any of this stuff," Sara said.

"Me, either. Is Winter in here?" Katrina forgot about her leg.

They walked to a tank with a dolphin and two young women. Katrina noticed a hula hoop, floating toys, and an air mattress in the water.

"That's right," the volunteer said, "and these are her trainers. She has physical therapy every day for two hours. Otherwise, she'll develop spine problems."

Katrina's dad rubbed his back. "Yep. Just like a person. What happened to her?"

"When she was a few months old, Winter caught her tail in a crab trap line," the volunteer explained.

"Fortunately, a nearby fisherman in a small boat noticed a commotion in the water. He checked it out and saw a baby dolphin in trouble. He cut her loose, but she was in bad shape, and her mother was nowhere around."

"Oh, no." Katrina said. "How did they catch her?"

"Well," the volunteer continued, "he and some other fishermen steered her into shallow water, where they comforted her until help came. A Sea World van brought her here, because it was the closest marine animal ambulance. We didn't see how she could live, especially after losing her tail."

The volunteer smiled and looked at Winter. "But you're a fighter, aren't you, girl?"

"Wow!" was all Katrina could say.

"Today," the volunteer continued, "she wears a prosthetic tail part of the day. Helps her backbone and lets her swim like a dolphin's supposed to swim."

Katrina felt her eyes widen. She caught her breath. *She's just like me. She's just like me.*

"Mom, I have to meet her," Katrina pleaded, staring at the young dolphin. "She'll understand exactly how I feel. We're like each other, only she has a helper tail!"

Her mother put an arm around Katrina's shoulder. "We'll have to wait until the dolphin demonstration's over. It's starting now. Let's grab those front row seats."

During the talk, a dolphin trainer held up Winter's prosthetic tail. "Does anyone know what this is?" she asked.

Katrina's hand shot up. "I do, because I have one, too. Not a tail. A leg."

"Oh, I see," the trainer said. "So you and Winter are a lot alike."

Katrina nodded. "Can I please meet her?"

"I think that can be arranged," the young woman said. "Stay here when we finish."

A few minutes after the performance ended, a tall man with a ready smile walked up to the Simpkins family. "Hi," he said. "I'm the aquarium's director. I hear one of you wants to meet Winter."

"That's me. I'm Katrina," she said. "She's so much like me. Please, I need to meet her."

"Hi, Katrina," He shook her hand. "Let's arrange that right away. A trainer will help, but if there's anything else I can do, let me know. Good luck to you and your family."

"Thank you," she said, solemnly.

A young woman, wearing a wet suit, came up the steps. "Hello, I'm Winter's trainer. I hear you want to meet our girl. Can you kneel over there on the platform?"

"I can. Kneeling rubs my leg a little, but I can do it. I want to do it." Katrina went to the platform and slowly knelt down.

The trainer smiled. "Great. Take your time. Good job. I'll call her over, and you two can get acquainted." She whistled and gave the dolphin a hand signal.

"OH MY GOSH!" Katrina said. "Here she comes! Right to me!" She patted the young dolphin and rubbed her head. Katrina squealed.

"She's splashing me. Can I splash her back?" she asked the trainer. "Absolutely," the young woman answered. "That's exactly what she wants!" *That* meeting was the beginning of Katrina's new life.

Chapter 2
THE BEGINNING OF A MIRACLE

Two days after returning home, Katrina made a decision. "I want to join Jump Rope Club," she informed her mom.

Her mother raised her eyebrows. "But K, you don't know how."

"Oh, that's easy," Katrina said. "You can teach me. Let's go buy a jump rope. Two, actually. I'm gonna learn Double Dutch."

"This isn't so hard," she told her mom and sister, after they returned from the store with jump ropes. She grinned and wiped sweat from her face. "How many times have I fallen so far? A million?"

Frowning, her mom said, "Sweetheart, you're not going to have any skin left on your knee. And your elbow's bleeding. Maybe we should give it up."

Katrina put her hands on her hips. "I'm not a quitter anymore, Mom. Winter does activities all the time, and I bet she gets plenty of bruises. I'm going to jump rope."

All the next day in school, Katrina had a bad case of butterflies, thinking about having to jump rope that afternoon. At 3:15 she joined dozens of her classmates in the gym. *I'm gonna do this. I can do this. Winter's a normal dolphin, and I'm a normal girl.*

Katrina was halfway in the line of kids, taking turns to jump. *So far, nobody's made a mistake. I gotta do this right and not be the first failure.*

"It's your turn, Katrina," the coach said, jolting her back to reality like a glass of ice water splashed in her face.

She felt a tremor of terror in her stomach as she walked to the rope. *Remember the rhythm*, she said to herself, swaying with the rope. *Now, jump!*

"Oh, no," she groaned, catching her foot. She fell. Hard. *You won't cry. You're not hurt*, Katrina, she told herself. *Get up and do it again.* Her cheeks were burning, and she felt sick to her stomach.

Jodi, one of her classmates, bent down. "I'll help you. This happens to me all the time. Happens to all of us."

"Thanks, Jodi," Katrina murmured. "I got caught."

She brushed off her clothes, fighting back tears. She faked a sneeze and brushed her eyes when covering her nose. *Gotta catch my breath.* She breathed quietly. "Can I try it again?" Katrina asked the coach, surprising herself.

"Of course," he said.

Relax, rhythm, relax, rhythm, Katrina thought, remembering what Sara had told her. She swayed to the rope. *Jump. I'm in!* she shouted to herself.

After two weeks of Jump Rope Club, Katrina tripped no more than the other kids. Within a month, she was jumping Double Dutch and not falling at all. "This is the first after school activity I've done," she told her sister, while they practiced in the driveway. "But is it gonna be the last? I don't think so!"

It snowed the next day, and Katrina's mom picked her up after Jump Rope Club. Pushing back her wet parka hood, Katrina looked at her mother. "I miss Winter so much. She understands me. I have to see her again!"

"But K," her mom answered, "We've talked about this. You know we can't afford another trip to Florida right now. There's a Shriner's Hospital visit to Chicago soon. It's almost time for a new prosthesis."

"I know, Mom." Katrina started to cry. "But she's changing my life. I have to thank her. Maybe I'm changing hers, too. And we met the director, and he wanted to help. And I need help to see Winter." She stopped for breath, sobbing between gulps of air.

Her mom sighed. "Alright, sweetheart. I'll call him and see if there's any way you can get back to visit Winter."

When they arrived home, Katrina's mother went up to her bedroom and shut the door. Katrina followed and soon heard her mom's muffled voice coming from behind the door. Katrina paced back and forth. *Please let him say yes. If only he can find a way to get me back to Winter!*

After what seemed forever to Katrina, the door opened. Her mom shot her a sunny smile. "Well Miss K, here's the scoop. The director's flying our family to Florida. How would you like to make a video with Winter?"

Katrina stared at her mom. "What? What did you say?"

"The aquarium wants to do a video about you and your prosthetic leg with Winter and her prosthetic tail," her mom explained. "It'll be used at the aquarium several times each day. He was going to call us tomorrow!"

"Yes!" Katrina shouted, arms in the air. "My dreams have come true, like in fairy tales. Only this is real life. I'm so excited! How can I wait? When are we going?" She stopped talking and looked at her mother. "Winter's helped me so much. Maybe I can start to help other people, but I gotta figure out how."

Chapter 3
NOT ONE BUTTERFLY AFRAID

On a blustery winter's morning two weeks later, a Shriner's Hospital van picked up Katrina and her parents for the trip to Chicago. "So a film crew's gonna be there, waiting for me?" Katrina asked her mom for the third time.

Her mother sighed. "K don't be nervous. You'll do fine. After all, you've been making this trip since you were ..."

"I know, Mom. Two months old. And I'm not nervous." *I'm really not.* She looked at at her palms. They weren't sweaty.

"Okay, Katrina," the driver said, pulling up to patient delivery. "I'll get the wheelchair."

"No, thanks," she said. "I'm walking to the door this time—and from now on."

"Oh, I don't …" her dad began.

Katrina held up her hand. "Please Dad, I need to do some things by myself."

She saw her mom and dad exchange glances. "Thanks, guys," she said, opening the door. She stepped out into the frigid air and walked carefully into the hospital.

The family was met in the lobby by Shriner's public relations director. "Hi, she said. "Great to meet you." She turned toward Katrina and smiled. "Ready for your adventure today?"

Katrina tucked a straggling curl behind her ear. She nodded. "Uh-huh. I'm gonna help kids by making this video."

The filming began with Katrina talking to her doctor. "You may need one more surgery," he said. "The good news is it can wait awhile. We won't rush into anything. That work for you?"

Katrina smiled. "Yeah. That's great news!"

"Okay, guys. Got it," Jake, one of the videographers announced. "Let's move on to the new prosthesis if everyone's ready."

The lights were in place, and once again the video started. Katrina stood between two handrails for support, while the technician fitted her new prosthesis. "Wow, you're having a growth spurt. It's definitely time for a new leg!"

Katrina leaned over to see the new prosthesis. "My pants were getting too short, so I knew!"

"Yep, kids have a way of surprising us by insisting on growing," the technician said, smiling.

"It's a wrap, as we say in show business," Jake said, giving Katrina a thumbs-up. "You've been a trooper today, kiddo."

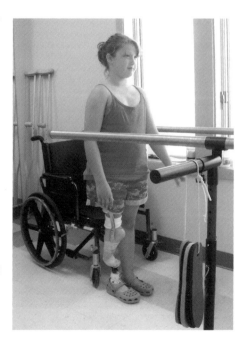

She laughed. "Thanks. I feel like a star. I'm gonna start dancing and singing." *I might, too,* she thought.

On the van ride back to Indiana, Katrina was thoughtful. *Could I really do stuff like that? Dance and sing? I've always wanted to. Maybe … some day.*

"Seventy two hours, twenty minutes," Katrina said to her friend, Bev, a week after returning from Shriner's Hospital. "You know what that means?"

"Uh, maybe something to do with Florida?" Bev answered. "Just a crazy guess on my part."

Katrina grinned and high-fived her. "Yup. Leaving to see Winter. But I'm not excited or anything."

Seventy-seven hours later, the Simpkins family landed at Tampa International Airport. Katrina's dad drove her straight to the Clearwater Marine Aquarium. He parked their rental car, and she walked in by herself.

"Hi, I'm Katrina Simpkins, and I'm here to see Winter," she told the lady behind the ticket counter.

The woman came around the desk and gave Katrina a hug. "It's nice to see you again, dear. You're expected upstairs."

Katrina grinned and pushed a pesky curl off her face. "Thanks. I'm so excited to be here. See you later." She walked toward the stairs, the thought of her prosthetic leg, struggling up the steps, bothered her not a bit.

When she saw the dolphin Katrina put her hands to her mouth. "Winter," she half-whispered, "I'm back."

"Hey, Katrina," the trainer called from the dolphin's tank. "Get into a wet suit and come on in. Our girl's waiting."

"Okay," she said, watching Winter watch her.

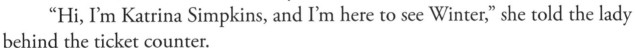

After changing into a wet suit, Katrina lowered herself into the tank and waited. The trainer said, "Here comes Winter. Wow! Does she know you, or what?"

"She's swimming right into my arms," a tearful Katrina said.

And the young dolphin stayed there while her friend whispered to her and stroked her head. "I've missed you so much," Katrina said softly.

The trainer smiled. "You guys are a lot alike. No wonder you're such good friends."

"Video crew's here!" the grey haired volunteer shouted to the trainer, breaking the spell.

"I have to go now, but I'll be back soon," Katrina told the dolphin. "We're doing a film together." *I can't believe any of this is happening.* She slowly lifted herself out of the water.

Long shadows stretched across the dolphin tanks when the filming finished. Katrina and several other special needs children, along with soldiers missing an arm or leg, had interacted with Winter for the video. They rubbed her belly and stroked her head. She let them inspect the area where her tail got caught.

This was the best day of my life. I never thought I'd be this happy. Today, I feel like a normal girl.

Next afternoon, the Simpkins family visited the aquarium again. Katrina's sister, Sara, shaded her eyes and looked around.

"Whoa, look at the crowd, K! We'd better snag a seat."

"Welcome, Ladies and Gentlemen and Kids," the announcer said. "It's great to have such a large group! You're going to see our dolphins do their daily demonstration. Hey, is that Katrina I see over there? You want to tell these nice folks all about our special dolphin? Here's her old prosthetic tail," she said, picking it up from a table. "Come on over and help us out."

"Oh, I can't," she began. *Wait a minute, why not? I have courage like Winter.* "Okay. Sure, I'd like to help." Katrina surprised herself again.

Walking to the podium, she discovered, *I'm not afraid. Not one little butterfly afraid.* She attached her head piece, looked at the audience, and smiled. "Hi. My name is Katrina Simpkins. I'm happy to talk about Winter. We're a lot alike."

Katrina held up the prosthetic tail and a white sleeve. "This was made by Hanger Prosthetic Company. It's really heavy, but it's the right weight for a dolphin her size. And they invented this soft sock to go under it."

She caught her breath. "Hanger made me a new leg, and they put a cool picture of Winter on it!"

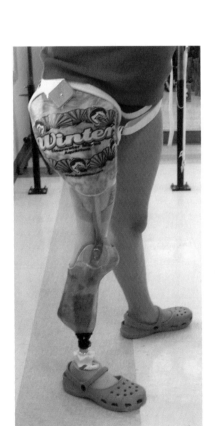

"So I have a helper leg, and Winter has a helper tail. I have to use one because of a birth defect, and hers—well, you know about hers. But we're both fine. And happy," she added, realizing she was.

After the dolphin demonstration, Katrina walked alone to Winter's tank. The young dolphin swam to Katrina, who knelt by the water. Stroking the dolphin's head, Katrina whispered, "Thanks for everything you've done for me. Saving my life and all. Maybe in a tiny way, I helped save yours."

Chapter 4
NORMAL IN VIEW

Upon returning home, Katrina became busier than ever. She joined her community's 4-H Club. One of her tasks was to show Brandy, the family dog. And they won a ribbon!

"Alright, you three winners," the judge said from the podium. "Come on up here and say a thing or two about your pooch."

When it was her turn, Katrina held up their Second Place red ribbon. "I knew Brandy could do it. She used to be such a shy dog, but she isn't anymore. This show gave her lots of confidence."

The next evening at dinner, Katrina made an announcement. "Hey, guys, Coach asked me to join the gymnastics group. I'm going for it."

"Oh, I'm not sure about that." Her dad put down his iced tea. "We'd better ask your doctor and Hanger Prosthetics."

She nodded. "Sure, we can ask, but I'm joining."

This time, everything was different. *These kids are my friends, and if I make a mistake, it'll be okay.* Katrina walked to the balance beam. This time, classmates cheered when she went through the routine flawlessly.

"Don't you guys love the balance beam?" she asked Bev and Jodi at the end of an after school gymnastics workout. "The stretches feel great—especially on my helper leg." She looked at the girls and laughed. "Gotcha! Hey, guys, is it weird because I like standing on my head?" Katrina asked the girls.

"Nope," Bev said. "You're just weird to begin with."

Katrina chuckled. "Yeah, that must explain it. Seriously, though, I feel normal when I practice my floor routine."

Bev frowned. "What do you mean you feel normal? You are normal."

Yeah, maybe I am.

The girls gathered up their gear, heading for the door. "Bye, guys," Jodi said, walking to her mom's car.

"See you tomorrow." Bev and Katrina waited for the bus.

Bev bumped her friend's arm. "You gotta get over this not feeling normal thing. Tell yourself, 'I am normal. I am normal.' Pretty soon you'll believe it."

"Yeah," Katrina said. "I try it all the time. But it's hard when people stare. Maybe I'd stare at me, too. I don't know."

Bev frowned. "Look K, your helper leg is part of who you are. On the gymnastics floor, you're great. It doesn't matter to your friends. Nada. Zero. Zip. Okay? Here comes the bus. Jump on. Pretend you're on the trampoline!"

Katrina's stop was first. She said goodbye to Bev and tried hard not to let the limp upset her, as she went down the steps and off the bus. *I'm not gonna let my limp bother me. But I'm gonna try walking without it, too.*

Katrina had made another decision. "I'm going to modeling school!" Katrina told Bev, as they walked to class next morning. "I saw a sign about it on the bus stop bench. Talked to my parents about it at breakfast, and they said yes. I'm gonna sign up, and I'll wear dresses, and skirts and not pants all the time."

"It's a great idea," her friend answered. "Go for it."

"Yeah, I can do it, the same as anybody, now that my prosthesis has a foot for heels, too. It'll be fun. "

After school, she found her mom and Sara in the kitchen. "Here's our invitation for the aquarium's gala!" She held a thick white envelope. "It came in the mail."

"That's exciting," Katrina's mom said. "We have to get you a new party dress, K. Long or short?"

"Red and short," she answered. "No more hiding my helper leg. It's part of me, and I'll be allergic to anyone who doesn't like me because of it."

"Woo Hoo. That's the spirit," Sara said, high-fiving her sister. "You've made my year!"

"Okay," Katrina said. "Now, let's go jump some rope."

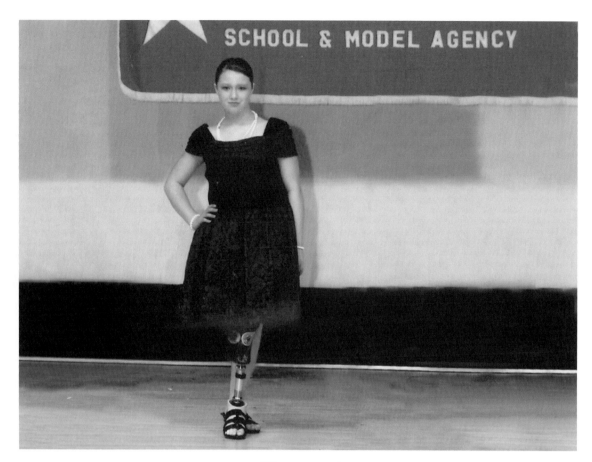

Chapter 5
A HERO'S LIFE

Katrina's dad lifted her suitcase from the conveyer belt at the Tampa Airport. Inside, carefully wrapped in tissue paper, was Katrina's short red party dress. "Let's go, gang. I've got everything. This'll be a great time for all of us— even Katrina," he said, winking at her.

She grinned. "Yep. I've gotta act grown-up tonight, whether I want to or not."

That evening, the family walked into the Sand Pearl Hotel on Clearwater Beach. "You look so beautiful, K." Sara watched photographers taking pictures of her sister. "Have fun."

Katrina gulped and ducked her head. "You know what? I'm nervous. I'd rather be with Winter!"

Sara grinned. "You're getting famous. Gotta deal with it!"

During the after dinner speeches, the director asked Katrina, "Well, what do you think of all this?"

She blushed. *I don't have any words to say how I feel. Maybe happy? That's it. I'm so happy.* But the words didn't come.

"Wow, Katrina, I haven't seen this side of you for a long time!" he said, laughing with the audience.

Soon after the family returned home from Florida, Katrina's life began to change. Newspapers got in touch, all wanting to do stories about her. And the emails began. At first it was one, then two, then a dozen a day. Then more, all forwarded to the Simpkins family by the aquarium. People were viewing Katrina's video at the Clearwater Marine Aquarium and were reaching out to her.

"You got your wish," Sara told Katrina. "You're helping so many people, Sis. I'm proud of you."

"It's all about Winter," Katrina would reply, answering emails that her parents had okayed. "She's everybody's inspiration."

Sara shook her head and smiled. "Typical K response."

"Here's a surprise response," Katrina answered. "I don't like having to be brave all the time and not worry what people think. I don't like being different, Sara." Her tears threatened again.

"But look how far you've come, Sis," she said, giving Katrina a hug. "Not long ago, you had a hard time looking at people when they talked to you. Now you speak in front of big groups. That's something I wouldn't do!"

Katrina stared at her sister. "I know, but …"

"Look K, you're so lucky. You've made your own luck. People respect you, and they want to be like you. They want to have your courage. Not many people can do it, but you can," Sara said, tears welling in her eyes. "You're everybody's hero. You definitely are mine."

"I do want to help people," Katrina said softly, "but it's hard to be me sometimes. I'm gonna keep on trying though. Like Winter tries. I promise to do that for you and for other people."

Epilogue

Katrina kept her word. She reached out to anyone who needed help. She was a role model for those with special needs and those without. She volunteered at a local charity to promote reading. She worked at a horse rescue farm and learned to ride and to jump.

She rode in the Shriner's Benefit Horse Shows. She took voice lessons, wrote songs, and performed them.

She spoke to many groups about overcoming a handicap. Katrina never forgot to mention Winter.

Katrina enrolled in modeling school, attended for two years, and graduated. She wore dresses or skirts and made a point of walking well in front of an audience.

Gone were the days when she would look no one in the eye.

When she would speak to no one.

When she was afraid to try anything new.

And gone was the self-doubt.

"I just want to be a normal somebody," Katrina once said.

She was that and so much more. She was courageous in ways most people never have to be. Every hour. Every day.

A hero's courage.

A hero's heart.

A normal girl called Katrina.

Author's Notes
Katrina and Winter

Katrina Simpkins was born with a birth defect called, Proximal femoral focal deficiency (PFFD). This condition caused Katrina's right leg to be shorter than her normal left one. Her right foot is much smaller as well. With her prosthesis, Katrina's legs are the same length, and she can do all the things you've read about in this biography.

Shriner's Hospitals are located throughout the US. They only treat children, and the treatment is free of charge. Each hospital has its own specialty. Katrina has been treated at both the Chicago and Tampa Shriner's Hospitals.

The Clearwater Marine Aquarium in Clearwater, Florida, did not begin as an aquarium. Originally, it was a sewage treatment plant. The tanks that were used for sewage waste were cleaned and made safe. They are now home to marine animals, such as dolphins and sea turtles.

The aquarium is home to both Winter and Hope, another young dolphin who was rescued after Winter. Both animals were found off the east coast of Florida, close to the Kennedy Space Station. They were brought to the Clearwater Marine Aquarium, because they know how to treat wounded or orphaned sea mammals.

Today, the Clearwater Marine Aquarium is a successful Florida destination. It has been enlarged with stadium seating for viewing and learning about dolphins. A large addition for animal research and a parking garage have been built.

CPSIA information can be obtained at www.ICGtesting.com
Printed in the USA
BVIW121203270519
548679BV00008B/8